WRITING BUSINESS
PROPOSALS AND REPORTS

Strategies for Success

Susan L. Brock

A FIFTY-MINUTE™ SERIES BOOK

CRISP PUBLICATIONS, INC.
Menlo Park, California

WRITING BUSINESS PROPOSALS AND REPORTS
Strategies for Success

Susan L. Brock

CREDITS:
Editor: **Beverly M. Manber**
Designer: **Carol Harris**
Typesetting: **ExecuStaff**
Cover Design: **Carol Harris**
Artwork: **Ralph Mapson**

Copyright © 1992 Crisp Publications, Inc.
Printed in the United States of America

Distribution to the U.S. Trade:

National Book Network, Inc.
4720 Boston Way
Lanham, MD 20706
1-800-462-6420

Library of Congress Catalog Card Number 91-76247
Brock, Susan L.
Writing Business Proposals and Reports
ISBN 1-56052-122-8

This book is printed on recyclable paper with soy ink.

ABOUT THIS BOOK

WRITING BUSINESS PROPOSALS AND REPORTS is not like most books. It stands out from other self-help books in an important way. It's not a book to read—it's a book to *use*. The unique "self-paced" format of this book and the many worksheets encourage the reader to get involved and try some new ideas immediately.

The objective of WRITING BUSINESS PROPOSALS AND REPORTS is to provide the reader with a basic understanding of how to write successful proposals and reports. By applying the information presented, the reader will be able to present organized, clear, concise reports or proposals.

WRITING BUSINESS PROPOSALS AND REPORTS can be used effectively in a number of ways. Here are some possibilities.

—Individual Study. Because the book is self-instructional, all that is needed is a quiet place, some time and a pencil. By completing the activities and exercises, a reader should not only receive valuable feedback, but also practical steps for self-improvement.

—Workshops and Seminars. The book is ideal for assigned reading prior to a workshop or seminar. With the basics in hand, the quality of the participation will improve, and more time can be spent on concept extensions and applications during the program. The book is also effective when it is distributed at the beginning of a session, and participants "work through" the contents.

—Remote Location Training. Books can be sent to those not able to attend "home office" training sessions.

There are several other possibilities that depend on the objectives, program or ideas of the user.

One thing is for sure, even after it has been read, this book will be looked at—and thought about—again and again.

i

CONTENTS

OVERVIEW

If you have ever stared at the blinking cursor on your computer screen (or worse, at a blank piece of paper in your typewriter), you know the anxieties involved in putting your thoughts on paper. In business, not only are we required to write the basic forms of communication (usually memos and letters), but we soon realize there is more to learn: how to write successful proposals and winning reports. Here are brief descriptions of each:

Proposals

A proposal's primary objective is to persuade your target audience to take specific action, including hiring you or your firm or buying your product. Often you will write a proposal in response to a Request for Proposal (RFP) sent to you by another organization.

To win a new client or customer or retain an existing one, you usually face strong competition. Whether you work for an organization or you are self-employed, proposal writing often presents a key opportunity for you to stand out from the crowd. A poorly written proposal can quickly kill your chances; a good one can influence—or even determine—the outcome.

That is why your proposal has to be as good as you can make it. Not only should it be clear and concise, but it must be persuasive and tailored for the potential client or customer.

Reports

You may need to write reports for readers internal or external to your organization, although you may find that most of your reports will be for someone in higher authority within your organization. People in business write reports for a variety of reasons. Reports can be informative or persuasive or a combination of both. Persuasive reports usually fall into two broad categories: (1) problem/solution and (2) feasibility studies. Informative reports include employee evaluations, progress reports and minutes of meetings.

Short reports (fewer than eight pages) are sometimes in a memo or letter format, while long reports are more formal and may include a title page and table of contents.

Writing winning proposals and successful reports requires knowing more than the fundamentals of writing well. In the following pages, you will learn how to organize, develop and edit your reports and proposals. You will learn that report and proposal writing is a process—not a single event. You will also discover strategies to help you tailor your work and persuade your reader, so you will be more successful in achieving your objectives.

P A R T

I

Strategies for Writing Proposals and Reports

WRITING SELF-ASSESSMENT

Before you begin to write, pause for a moment. Think about what you do well in writing and what you would like to improve. For example, you might feel comfortable with your knowledge of the fundamentals of good writing (more on this later), but you might not be sure how to write persuasively.

For the next few moments, think about your own skills and assess your writing ability. This exercise will help you focus on specifics. It will give you direction to improve the skills you possess or to acquire the skills you would like to possess.

My specific writing strengths are:

1. _____

2. _____

3. _____

4. _____

5. _____

SELF-ASSESSMENT (continued)

My specific writing weaknesses are:

1. _____

2. _____

3. _____

4. _____

5. _____

Refer to this inventory of your writing skills as you read this book. We will begin with how you can become a more effective writer by thinking about *strategy*.

Strategy comes before you even begin to write. And strategy is one of the most neglected elements in the writing process.

REVIEWING THE BASICS

Perhaps the most basic strategy in writing has to do with writing basics, such as spelling, grammar, punctuation and mechanics. Nothing distracts a reader more or reduces your credibility faster than a report or proposal filled with mechanical errors. If you have trouble with the basics (and you know who you are!), take steps now to improve. Enroll in an evening course at your local community college, or buy a book written to help with the basics of writing. It is never too late to learn to write well.

If your basic writing skills are generally strong, but you have trouble remembering some of the finer points of writing, the next few pages should provide a handy review.

PUNCTUATION POINTERS

The Comma [,]

The comma sets off or separates words or groups of words within sentences.

1. Use a comma after a long introductory phrase or clause: ''After arriving to work late, I went immediately into the meeting.''

2. If the introductory material is short, forget the comma: ''After lunch I introduced the new director to my boss.''

3. But use a comma if the sentence would be confusing without it: ''After eating, the snake curled up and went to sleep.''

4. Use a comma to separate items in a series: ''My job requires writing, effective speaking, regular delegating, and supervising employees.'' (Note: The comma before the conjunction is optional.)

5. Use a comma to separate independent clauses that are joined by a conjunction (*and, but, or, nor, for, so, yet*). ''We went to the meeting, but no one had arrived.'' or ''We worked long and hard, yet the work kept piling up.''

6. Use a comma(s) to set off *nonessential* information in a sentence. Compare these two sentences:

   ''Frank, wearing a pinstripe suit, left for the client's office.'' [*Wearing a pinstripe suite* adds nonessential information about Frank.]

   ''The client wearing the pinstripe suit is ready to meet with you now.'' [Here, *wearing a pinstripe suit* identifies which client is ready. This sentence implies that more than one client is there.]

PUNCTUATION POINTERS (continued)

The Semicolon [;]

The semicolon separates two thoughts, linking those two thoughts more closely than a period can. ''I drafted the logo; my assistant designed it.''

The following words require a semicolon *before* and a comma *after,* if the words come between two separate thoughts:

accordingly	hence	moreover	similarly
also	however	namely	still
besides	likewise	nevertheless	then
consequently	indeed	nonetheless	therefore
furthermore	instead	otherwise	thus

''I thought my assistant had completed the tax return; consequently, I was surprised when I found the tax file on my desk.''

''We have canceled the staff's retreat this winter; instead, we will reschedule it for next spring.''

The Colon [:]

A colon tells the reader that more information is coming: a list, a long quotation or an explanation. It is used to separate independent thoughts when the second thought explains the first.

''It's safe to predict what health care costs will do next year: they will go up.''

The Apostrophe ['']

An apostrophe forms the possessive of nouns and some pronouns, and it replaces missing letters in contractions.

''I learned a lot from *Brian's* presentation.''

''*Someone's* coat is in the lobby.''

''The *Joneses'* tax return is on my desk.''

''Why *don't* you let Ted help you with this project?''

Use an apostrophe with letters mentioned as letters:

''Be sure to dot your *i's* and cross your *t's* in this memo.''

But you usually do not need an apostrophe with abbreviations:

''The CPAs decided to attend the continuing education class to learn more about HMOs [health maintenance organizations].''

COMMON FAULTS

Along with *basic* problems in business writing are these four common faults:

1. Too many words
2. Clichés
3. Too many big words
4. *I* perspective

Here is a description of each:

1. Too Many Words

A common fault of many writers is that they use more words than they need to express an idea. A good way to improve this is to write freely in the first draft, then edit, edit, edit. Eliminate any word that doesn't serve a purpose.

For example:

Before: This note is to let you know that we are sponsoring a company picnic next month in Lincoln Grove. If you need directions, please don't hesitate to contact us.

Revised: ~~This note is to let you know that~~ We are sponsoring a company picnic next month in Lincoln Grove. If you need directions, please ~~don't hesitate~~ contact us.

After: We are sponsoring a company picnic next month in Lincoln Grove. If you need directions, please contact us.

Notice that the *after* version is more concise. Here is another example:

Before: In the event of a hiring freeze, in the majority of instances we will not be required to lay off any of our staff.

Revised: ~~In the event of~~ a hiring freeze, ~~in the majority of instances~~ we will not have to lay off ~~any of our~~ staff.

After: If we have a hiring freeze, we will not have to lay off staff.

Don't be afraid to edit ruthlessly when you write. You will find that your writing is clearer and more vigorous.

Editing Redundant Expressions Exercise

Redundant Expressions: Sometimes people use too many words because of redundant phrases. Many redundant phrases sound right because we hear them often, but look at the list below and line through all unnecessary words in each expression. The first two are already lined through for you:

~~advance~~ planning

ask ~~a question~~

as to whether

as yet

at a later date

at the present time

basic fundamentals

specific example

but nevertheless

close proximity

close scrutiny

combine together

completely empty

consensus of opinion

continue on

exact opposites

first of all

for a period of 10 days

just exactly

my personal opinion

absolutely essential

refer back

true facts

whether or not

written down

brief moment

on a regular basis

period of time

recur again

thorough investigation

sufficient enough

started off with

merged together

repeat again

(Compare your answers with those of the author on the next page.)

COMMON FAULTS (continued)

Following are the author's answers from the exercise on page 11.

~~advance~~ planning

ask ~~a question~~

~~as to~~ whether

~~as~~ yet

~~at a~~ later date

at ~~the~~ present ~~time~~

~~basic~~ fundamentals

~~specific~~ example

~~but~~ nevertheless

~~close~~ proximity

~~close~~ scrutiny

combine ~~together~~

~~completely~~ empty

consensus ~~of opinion~~

continue ~~on~~

~~exact~~ opposites

first ~~of all~~

for ~~a period of~~ 10 days

~~just~~ exactly

my ~~personal~~ opinion

~~absolutely~~ essential

refer ~~back~~

~~true~~ facts

whether ~~or not~~

written ~~down~~

~~brief~~ moment

~~on a~~ regular ~~basis~~

period ~~of time~~

recur ~~again~~

~~thorough~~ investigation

sufficient ~~enough~~

started ~~off~~ with

merged ~~together~~

repeat ~~again~~

2. Clichés

One reason we use too many words is that we use expressions that are *overused*. Clichés compound our writing faults because they are trite expressions that add unnecessary words. Here is an example:

Before: Please be advised that at the present time we have no available job openings. Thank you for your consideration.

After: Currently we have no job openings. Thank you.

Here is a list of other clichés you have probably heard:

enclosed please find   at a later date
per your request   at the present time
consensus of opinion   close proximity
at your earliest convenience each and every one
last but not least   tried and true

Do these phrases sound familiar?

Cliché Exercise

Now it is your turn to recognize and recast clichés. Read the following paragraph and circle all clichés:

As per our telephone conversation, enclosed please find two copies of our agreement. Please read this information at your earliest possible convenience— but before our meeting on Tuesday. After you have an opportunity to review this agreement, please call me. Thank you for your consideration.

On the following lines, rewrite the paragraph and omit the clichés.

_____

_____

_____

_____

_____

_____

CLICHÉS (continued)

Below is a revised version of the paragraph you were asked to rewrite on page 13. Although your rewritten paragraph may be different from the one below, your writing will improve if you avoid those phrases that sound very familiar—clichés.

Revised Version:

As you requested, I am enclosing two copies of our agreement. Please review this information before next Tuesday's meeting. After you review this agreement, please call me. Thank you for your help.

3. Too Many Big Words

Many people choose to use big words when they write because they believe it makes them sound impressive. These folks write to impress, not to express. Instead of choosing the best word for what they want to say, they choose the most impressive (or biggest) word. Look at the differences in these pairs of sentences:

1. *Prior to departure, please terminate the illumination.*

or

2. *Before you leave, please turn off the lights.*

3. *The plumber discovered an excessive moisture condition in the bathroom pipes.*

or

4. *The plumber discovered a leak in the bathroom pipes.*

5. *Further notification will follow this correspondence.*

or

6. *I'll keep you informed.*

Your writing will be better if you write simply and naturally. Read your reports and proposals aloud after you write to *hear* if they sound natural and conversational.

4. ''I'' Perspective

Proposals and reports will be more effective if you use *you* more than you use *I*. Your proposals will be more persuasive if you concentrate on writing from the reader's perspective: people want to know how *they* will benefit.

Here is how to test your writing: after you finish a proposal or report, count the number of times you have used the following words: you, your, yours. Next, count how often you use these words: me, us, I, we. The more you use *you, your* or *yours,* the more likely your writing will convey your concern for your reader's needs.

For example, read the following sentences to see who the message emphasizes:

or

    1. *Our copier makes the best copies on the market today.*

    2. *Your copies will be the best you've seen, when you use our copier.*

If you help your readers discover how they will benefit, they will quickly see the advantages of buying your product or using your services.

''I'' Perspective Exercise

Read the following and circle all *me, us, I, we* pronouns; then, recast the sentences to convey *you, your* or *yours* and to reduce the I perspective.

We are pleased to describe our consulting services and we are committed to delivering the highest quality services to your company.

We believe that our firm is the best choice for your organization because:

- *We have served as your computer consultants for the past five years*
- *We have strong data processing and communications capabilities*
- *We have a large and expert local staff*
- *Our long-standing relationship with you permits us to more thoroughly know your people, products, and organizational structure*

We believe that the attached proposal will convince you that we are the best consultants to meet your needs.

"I" PERSPECTIVE (continued)

Now it is your turn. Write your revised version in the space below.

_____

_____

_____

_____

_____

_____

_____

_____

_____

_____

_____

_____

_____

_____

_____

Compare your revision with the one on the facing page. Yours may be different; just remember that if you eliminated the majority of _I_ perspective pronouns and substituted _You,_ your writing will be geared to your reader.

Revision to "I" Perspective Exercise

Thank you for the opportunity to describe our consulting services. Successful completion of your project requires a well qualified team that provides responsive service. We are committed to delivering these timely and professional services to you.

To help ensure the success of this project, our consultants bring extensive knowledge and experience to your company because of our:

- *Experience as your computer consultants for the past five years*
- *Strong data processing and communications capabilities*
- *Large and experienced local staff*
- *Long-standing relationship with you, which permits us to more thoroughly know your people, products and organization structure*

The attached proposal describes our understanding of your needs and our ability to meet those needs.

OTHER SUGGESTIONS TO SHARPEN YOUR WRITING SKILLS

Avoid Jargon

Simply said, jargon is *shoptalk*—special words, terms or acronyms found in the workplace.

Recently, the computer industry contributed several jargon words to our language: parameters, interface, input and paradigm. Words ending in *ize* can also sound like jargon: utilize, optimize, maximize, prioritize and potentialize.

At best, jargon is a shorthand way to communicate with those in your field; at worst, jargon can sound pretentious and can confuse your reader. Here are some examples:

Before: The company expanded its medical coverage to include HMOs and PPOs.

After: The company expanded its medical coverage to include Health Maintenance Organizations and Preferred Provider Organizations.

Before: Our operator will interface with the communication systems network.

After: Our operator will answer the telephones.

Before: The important information you will need to read is indicated by the dingbats.

After: The important information you need is indicated by the dashes (or bullets or asterisks).

If you are not sure how much your reader knows about the special terms particular to your industry, it is better to substitute more common expressions.

Preparing to Write

PREPARING TO WRITE

Before you write, think about your objectives. What specifically do you hope to accomplish? Remember that writing is a process. Here are some tips to help you get started.

1. Know your product or service. Explain why a prospect should select your firm or your product over your competitor's.

2. Know your prospect. Understand your customer's particular business needs and objectives before you can tailor your proposal to meet those needs.

3. Know the desired action. Determine what you want to achieve. If you want someone to do something (such as call you, complete and return the postage-paid card, or stop by your office), you will need to clearly convey the action you have in mind.

4. Write your first draft freely and quickly. Plan to edit and refine later. At least you will not be thinking, ''This first draft must be perfect.'' Nothing inhibits a writer more than trying for perfection too early. Writing quickly and freely will give you a positive feeling of progress.

5. Write the easy stuff first. Write what you can; then fill in the missing information. You will probably find that what seemed difficult at first, seems easier now—and less time-consuming.

PREPARING TO WRITE (continued)

We will look more closely at the first two items listed on page 19.

It probably seems obvious that you have to **know your product or your service** to be able to convince your customers that you can satisfy their needs. But knowing the merits of a product or service is only part of the reason people buy. Instead, consider *using* your knowledge to give your customers real reasons for buying. You have to know your product or service well enough to be able to demonstrate that it will benefit your customer.

Along with knowing your product or service, you must **know your prospect** and his or her needs. For example, if a young man drives to your car dealership in a sports car, you might automatically assume he wants to look at a newer sports car model. Suppose, however, he and his wife just had a baby, and he came to look at mid-size cars or station wagons. If you take the time to find out why he is looking, you can use that knowledge to show him larger models and give him even more reasons to buy.

Perhaps the most important suggestion is this: *Mentally prepare to write.* Here are some suggestions to help you:

1. Write when you can think clearly. For some folks, mornings are best. Others prefer to work at night. Try to work during the time that is best for you.

2. Recognize that you will have days when you are thinking clearly and days when your brain is foggy; try to allow enough flexibility in your schedule to tackle the difficult sections on your clear days.

3. Eliminate outside interruptions. If possible, close your door and forward your telephone calls, especially if you are trying to write a difficult section.

4. Visualize your finished product; then backtrack and jot down the steps you will need to take to complete your project.

5. Write your primary objective. Ask yourself these two questions: ''What is the specific reason I am writing?'' and ''What exactly do I hope to accomplish?'' These questions will create a focus for your project.

And now that you are ready, you can begin to organize your thoughts.

ORGANIZING FOR MAXIMUM IMPACT

The first way to help reduce the anxiety of facing a blank computer screen is to think SMALL. In other words, do not feel overwhelmed by thinking of the whole proposal or whole report, but break the whole into parts. Generally, the best structure is a simple one.

The following suggestions can help you organize your writing:

1. Tell your reader how the material is organized.

2. Write in A-B-C order (that is, sequentially).

3. Keep the number of sections to five or fewer.

4. Include each important piece of information only once and in the right place.

5. Use headings. They help you organize your thoughts and ideas, so that you can explain them clearly and sequentially.

6. If your proposal or report is over eight pages, consider adding an executive summary, sometimes called an introductory letter, at the beginning. The executive summary includes your best points expressed clearly, concisely and favorably.

It is easier to write a report or proposal that is broken into sections, and it is also easier to read. Your readers will not have to wade through a lot of information at once. They can read or simply skim the parts they want.

Organizing Reports

As you begin the report-writing process, you will need to decide which format to use: memo, letter or formal. Here are suggestions for each:

Letter format: For someone external to your company, and your report has fewer than eight pages.

Memo format: For someone inside your company, and your report has fewer than eight pages.

Formal format: For someone inside your company who is higher in authority, and your report is over eight pages long.

THE PERSUASIVE REPORT

If you are writing a **persuasive report** (such as a problem-solution study), think about strategy and consider organizing your report along the lines described below in ''The Motivated Sequence'' Outline:

The Motivated Sequence Outline

Attention—*arouses your readers' interest*

Need—*shows how the problem affects your readers*

Satisfaction—*offers a solution that resolves or reduces the problem*

Visualization—*shows how your readers will benefit by adopting the solution*

Action—*tells your readers specifically what they can do*

The Motivated Sequence Outline uses structure to build a case and lead a reader to take appropriate action. It makes your information even more compelling than it would be had you structured your report any other way. Each step of this outline builds upon the previous step. If you satisfy all steps, you will have established a need for change that your reader will want to act on.

Even if you do not recognize the structure of the Motivated Sequence, you will probably recognize the message conveyed in many sales letters. The Motivated Sequence Outline (or a similar version of it) is often used in sales presentations and proposals. Notice how it is used in the sales letter shown on the facing page.

```
                        ELITE TRAVEL AGENCY
                        333 CALIFORNIA STREET
                        SAN FRANCISCO, CA 94111


April 19, 19XX

Ms. Kathleen Atwood
204 London Street
Oakland, CA 94605

Dear Ms. Atwood:
```

(ATTENTION)   If you don't like romance, beautiful places, and friendly people, stop reading now.

(NEED)   But, if you need to get away from the pressures of work and school... if you would enjoy the exhilaration of bicycling through green pastures and rustic villages...if you want to be welcomed with open arms by a people known for their warm hospitality...then a guided bicycle tour through Ireland, one of Europe's most breathtaking countries, is for you.

(SATISFACTION)   Elite Travel is offering discount prices for students—like you—who wish to spend a splendid summer vacation experiencing a new culture in a foreign land--at prices so low, you can't afford to pass it up. Prices for 10-day tours begin at only $1,979, including airfare, bike rentals, 3 meals per day and lodging.

(VISUALIZATION)   Imagine bicycling on well maintained trails, stopping at points of historical interest and incredible views including castles, battlegrounds and lands where old Irish tales come to life. Each day we'll stop, tired and happy, at favorite bed and breakfast inns for deliciously prepared meals, hot baths and luxuriating sleep.

(ACTION)   If this package sounds good, call us today. Join us for a vacation you will talk about for years to come. Call toll free at 1-800-638-0900 before this offer ends on April 30. Don't miss out! We are going to have a great summer, and we'd love to have you along.

```
Sincerely,



Dan Edwards
Manager
```

In Part II of this book, you will find an example of a report that follows the "Motivated Sequence" Outline.

THE MOTIVATED SEQUENCE OUTLINE (continued)

Although developing each step of the outline is important, a well written "Attention" paragraph is crucial to encourage reading through the "Action" paragraph. Many people, however, find it difficult to write the important opening paragraph to any report or proposal. Once you successfully develop your opening ideas, it often seems that the remaining thoughts flow more naturally.

To give you practice in writing an attention-getting opening paragraph, here is an exercise. Let's say that you are opening a gourmet cafe that serves breakfast and lunch on a university campus. In the space below write an opening paragraph that introduces your cafe. Remember, your goal in the Attention paragraph is to arouse the interest of both students and university faculty.

_____

_____

_____

_____

_____

_____

_____

_____

_____

_____

_____

_____

_____

_____

After you finish writing your paragraph, turn the page to see alternative ways of developing an attention step of the Motivated Sequence.

Sample "Attention" Paragraphs

Dear Students and Faculty:

Are you tired of eating the same old greasy hamburger and fries? Or dried out vending machine food? Does eating on campus remind you of eating on an airplane? Well, prepare for a change!

Announcing the opening of *Campus Cuisine,* the first gourmet cafe that offers tantalizing tastes for finite finances.

Dear Students and Faculty:

Imagine walking to class and experiencing the aroma of freshly baked breads and hearty flavorful soups. Now, imagine sitting at a cozy table enjoying a rare roast beef sandwich, or spinach and lentil soup with a fresh sourdough baguette, or grilled swordfish with fennel and sun-dried tomatoes.

Campus Cafe is now open--right here on campus--to prepare for you a variety of delicious dishes at just-right prices.

FEASIBILITY STUDY

Another kind of report you may have to write is a **feasibility study**. To help you organize your thoughts, outline it first using the following headings:

Feasibility Study Outline

Overview—*main purpose; objectives*
Background—*supporting information; scope*
Project Details—*approach, findings, analysis*
Conclusions—*summarizes project*
Recommendations—*suggested action based on conclusions*

Using headings in a feasibility study breaks your report into manageable sections as you develop it. The easy-to-follow structure will help your reader better understand and appreciate your main ideas.

Part II contains an example of a feasibility study that follows the headings described above.

Organizing Proposals

If you are writing a proposal, your primary challenge is to show how the client or customer will benefit by choosing your company. You will need to show how well you have communicated your understanding of the client's business, your sensitivity to the client's needs, and your ability to respond to those needs quickly and creatively.

Following is one way to organize proposals:

- State the proposal's purpose and your company's interest in working with the prospective client.
- Describe your understanding of the prospect's company and industry.
- Explain your company's approach to providing the proposed services.
- Introduce the people who will do the work.
- Estimate the costs involved and the timeframe for the work.
- If necessary, include an appendix for supporting information.

By following a strategy when you organize your writing, you can clarify your message and encourage your reader to continue reading: two crucial components to persuading your reader.

Organizing Exercise

Here is an opportunity to test your knowledge! Read the following short report. Each paragraph is numbered, so all you need to do is read the report and renumber any paragraphs to make the report more cohesive. After you finish, turn to the next page and check your response with the author's.

MEMORANDUM

TO: STEVE JOHNSON

FROM: CAROLYN CARTER

DATE: SEPTEMBER 13, 19XX

RE: REPORT ON NEW SEMINAR: "HOW TO MARKET OUR SERVICES"

(1) _____ *The idea of having a course like this is excellent, and I think part of the course as it exists now is useful. On the other hand, this course could be much more worthwhile if it were structured differently.*

(2) _____ *As you requested, I recently attended the course called "How to Market Our Services."*

(3) _____ *First, reorganize the course to make it one full day instead of three half days. It tries to be too ambitious now and, as a result, it's fragmented.*

(4) _____ *For the last part of the day, have representatives from each area of business provide more general overviews of what they do and how we can use them—anecdotes help a lot. Learning more about our services is an extremely useful part of the course, but some of the presentations now are far too technical and detailed to appeal to an audience not working in that line of business.*

(5) _____ *For the first part of the day, teach the participants basic sales skills. Perhaps add videotape dramatizations on how to approach a client or prospective client.*

(6) _____ *I hope my suggestions help. I've developed a number of courses, and I'm convinced this course would be excellent if it were restructured and reorganized.*

(7) _____ *You might also add some case studies that are relevant to everyone. The case studies we're using now are more relevant for the personnel department, but to those of us in accounting and finance, they're less helpful.*

(8) _____ *Let me know if you'd like my help in restructuring this seminar to make it more useful to others in the company.*

REVISION TO ORGANIZING EXERCISE

Here is one way to make this report more cohesive. Notice how the ideas flow, and it has a clearer beginning, middle and end?

MEMORANDUM

TO: STEVE JOHNSON

FROM: CAROLYN CARTER

DATE: SEPTEMBER 13, 19XX

RE: REPORT ON NEW SEMINAR: "HOW TO MARKET OUR SERVICES"

~~(2)~~ __(1)__   *As you requested, I recently attended the course called "How to Market Our Services."*

~~(1)~~ __(2)__   *The idea of having a course like this is excellent, and I think part of the course as it exists now is useful. On the other hand, this course could be much more worthwhile if it were structured differently.*

(3)   *First, reorganize the course to make it one full day instead of three half days. It tries to be too ambitious now and, as a result, it's fragmented.*

~~(5)~~ __(4)__   *For the first part of the day, teach the participants basic sales skills. Perhaps add videotape dramatizations on how to approach a client or prospective client.*

~~(4)~~ __(5)__   *For the last part of the day, have representatives from each area of business provide more general overviews of what they do and how we can use them—anecdotes help a lot. Learning more about our services is an extremely useful part of the course, but some of the presentations now are far too technical and detailed to appeal to an audience not working in that line of business.*

~~(7)~~ __(6)__   *You might also add some case studies that are relevant to everyone. The case studies we're using now are more relevant for the personnel department, but to those of us in accounting and finance, they're less helpful.*

~~(6)~~ __(7)__   *I hope my suggestions help. I've developed a number of courses, and I'm convinced this course would be excellent if it were restructured and reorganized.*

(8)   *Let me know if you'd like my help in restructuring this seminar to make it more useful to others in the company.*

You may have noticed that this short report did not have headings. Headings are optional if your report is short and includes a subject line.

CHOOSING AN APPROPRIATE TONE

Have you heard the saying, "It's not what you say, but how you say it that's important?" Not only is this true for speakers, it is also true for writers. The tone of your message tells the reader a lot about you. For example, following are some subtle indicators that help establish your tone, for better or worse:

Condescending statements: Don't talk down to your reader. Writers sometimes do this because they have unintentionally chosen words that convey a condescending tone. For example, the words "of course" or "as you probably know" can convey "as any idiot knows."

Or you might be tempted to write something like this: "We all want to be better citizens and do our part to help reduce pollution." This kind of statement might sound preachy and self-righteous.

Sexist statements: Years ago people were taught that the pronouns "he, him, and his" were both masculine as well as neutral. Now, writers are more sensitive to others' perceptions of sexism, and they are careful about indiscriminately using the traditional neutral pronouns. For example, a traditional sentence might appear like this:

A CEO's effectiveness is measured, in part, by how well he develops his conceptual skills.

"He" and "his" are supposed to be neutral, but many people believe using the masculine pronouns in this case would suggest that CEOs are necessarily male.

Here is another way of looking at pronouns. Which of the following sentences are we more likely to see?

> *A nurse is trained to help his patients.*

or

> *A nurse is trained to help her patients.*

> *A good secretary does his work efficiently.*

or

> *A good secretary does her work efficiently.*

CHOOSING AN APPROPRIATE TONE
(continued)

If we choose a traditionally neutral pronoun, we would use ''his'' in both examples. But we are probably just as likely to use ''her'' only because the stereotypical nurse and secretary are women. For the same reasons as with our CEO example, nurses and secretaries are not necessarily female.

To avoid sexism, some writers choose the more cumbersome ''his or her'' or ''his/her.'' A better way to avoid sexist writing is to use plurals or restructure the sentences as in these examples.

Nurses are trained to help their patients.

or

A good secretary works efficiently.

By thinking about the sensitivities of your readers, you can communicate clearly and still structure your sentences so that they avoid appearing sexist.

Formal vs informal language: In years past, business writing was more formal—some say it was developed during the Victorian era. For example, people generally did not use the personal pronouns ''I'' or ''you,'' and they did not use contractions in formal writing.

While some businesses still require a more formal written style, most organizations now attempt to write more conversationally and naturally. With the increasing number of computers used to prepare proposals and reports, we need to make sure that our writing does not sound automated. Here are some suggestions for making your writing sound less formal:

1. Use contractions.

2. Use shorter, simpler words (for example, use ''about'' instead of ''approximately''; ''do'' instead of ''accomplish''; and ''show'' instead of ''demonstrate'').

3. Apply the conversation test. Read your writing aloud to *hear* how it sounds.

Negative expressions: When you are reviewing your report or proposal, see how many times you have used the words ''no'' or ''not.'' Then see how you have structured the sentences that contain those words. For example, read how each of these sentences sounds either positive or negative:

1. *We're sorry to tell you that we do not carry ABC software.*

or

2. *Because we no longer carry ABC software, we are sending you a list of distributors who do.*

The first sentence tells what you do not have or cannot do; the second sentence finishes by providing good news (and ends positively).

3. *Pete did not arrive on time, and he did not pay attention to what the salesperson said.*

or

4. *Pete arrived late, and he disregarded what the salesperson said.*

The first sentence describes Pete's behavior using negative terms (''not''); the second sentence describes Pete's behavior similarly but uses more neutral terms—and it is more specific and concise.

To convey a more positive tone when you write, try to choose neutral-to-positive words.

USING A CONSISTENT STYLE

The characteristics of your writing make up your writing style. Generally, the less attention you attract to the way you write, the more attention you will draw to what you say. Often, business writing seems cold and impersonal—due, in part, to the *tone* of it as you read in the previous section. And *tone* is part of style.

Why do we need to think about style? Here are four reasons:

1. A crisp, clear style permits easier reading.

2. Your final written product becomes more cohesive and coherent.

3. Style adds symmetry and rhythm to writing.

4. Your style tells your reader something about you as a human.

Here are two examples of a *breezy* style:

> *So, the next time you're in town, why don't ya swing by and look us up?*
>
> *You've got to like the ''bottom line'' appeal of our products.*

Sentences such as these two would be more appropriate as dialogue in a novel or as comments in an informal note to a close friend. Neither sentence, however, would be appropriate in a business proposal or report.

When you apply the conversation test to see if your writing is conversational and natural, make sure you do not sound flippant and breezy as the two sentences above suggest.

Another style in writing that some business people adopt is *stuffy* or *stilted*. In fact, many people would call traditional business writing ''stuffy.'' Here are two examples:

> *The aforementioned information should be sufficient to address your concerns.*
>
> *Subsequently, we will require your endorsement.*

You can improve these stuffy sentences by writing them this way:

> *The information above should answer your questions.*
>
> *Later we'll need your signature.*

Your writing will improve if you work toward a crisp, clear and simple style; then you will know that what you say is not obscured by how you say it.

EDITING TO ENHANCE YOUR WRITING

After you complete the first draft of your proposal or report, you will need to read it again and revise your work. Why edit? Here are a few reasons:

- Saves time by allowing you to draft more freely. You will know you can always go back and revise your work.

- Allows more thorough review with more objectivity—especially if you take a break from your work before you begin to edit.

- Results in a better finished product.

When you review your work, ask yourself these questions:

- Did I accomplish my objective? Did I do what my boss requested?

- Did I sufficiently cover the subject?

- Is the report logical and thorough?

- Did I anticipate my reader's objections and address them?

- Did I explain any unclear terms and references?

- Is the report easy to read and understand?

- Did I use a lot of white space to make the report more readable?

This last item, white space, means that you have used bullets (•), dashes, numbers, etc. to highlight key ideas instead of putting all information in paragraph form. Effective use of white space will encourage your reader to do just that: *READ*.

EDITING EXERCISE

To give you practice in editing skills, following are three wordy, stuffy sentences that need editing. Read each sentence; then write your revision in the space below. When you finish, compare your revisions with those of the author.

1. It has been my wish for a considerable period of time to gain entrance into the field of accounting. This is due to the fact that challenges of my intellect are what challenge me.

2. To me it appears that Smith did not give any attention whatsoever to the suggestion that had been recommended by the consultant.

3. In the past there were quite a large number of firms offering us competition. At this present point in time, the majority of those firms have been forced to go out of business by the hardships and difficulties of the present recessionary period of business contraction and stagnation.

Following are possible revisions. Your revisions may be different, but just remember that if you have eliminated unnecessary words and retained the meaning, you will have improved the sentences in this exercise—and that is what editing is all about!

1. I have always wanted to go into accounting because I find it challenging.

2. I believe that Smith disregarded the consultant's suggestion.

3. Much of our traditional competition has gone out of business because of the recession.

P A R T

II

Writing Successful Reports

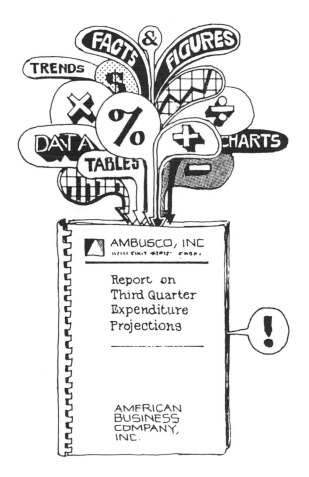

DEVELOPING YOUR IDEAS

Now that you have learned ways to organize reports, this chapter will help you develop your outlines into completed drafts. For purposes of this chapter, we will use the following headings in our report:

1. Overview, which may include background information

2. Statement of the problem

3. Proposed solution

4. Advantages and disadvantages of solution, which may include discussion of rejected alternatives

5. Conclusion/recommendation

Our job now is to develop each section.

Overview

This section serves as an introduction and tells the reader why you have written the report. Depending on the complexity of your report, you might need to provide background information. Ask yourself this question:

How much does the reader know about the situation discussed in this report?

If your supervisor asks you to write the report, you will not need to provide as much background information as you would in an unsolicited report.

A FOUR STEP PROCESS

1. Statement of the Problem

Get to the point quickly by clearly and concisely describing the problem.

2. Proposed Solution

Offer a clear and complete solution to the problem you have just described. After your research, you may discover that your solution does not solve the problem, but it does significantly reduce the problem, which may be all that is needed.

3. Pros and Cons of the Solution

To show that you have done your homework, describe the advantages as well as disadvantages of adopting your solution. Your primary objective here is to show that the advantages of adopting your solution outweigh the disadvantages.

For example, you recommend that your company purchase more computers from Company A to solve inventory problems. In your pros and cons section, you explain that Company B also has computers—and they are less expensive than Company A's. But Company A has a better service agreement and a greater variety of software. And it is these two reasons that support your recommendation to purchase computers from Company A—you have attempted to show that the advantages of better service and more software outweigh the disadvantage of paying more money with the initial purchase.

4. Conclusion

Summarize the main points of your report. List your points sequentially—that is, the way they appeared in the report. Provide only information that has already appeared in the report. Conclusions should not introduce new information.

Beginning on the facing page is an example of a memorandum report that is organized according to the five headings listed on page 39.

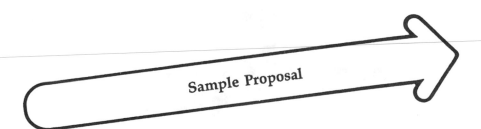

Sample Proposal

SAMPLE REPORT

MEMORANDUM

TO: Stewart Jensen, CEO

FROM: Gary Pence

DATE: October 23, 19XX

RE: Report to Reduce Communication Problems and Increase Sales

Overview

Last quarter, our sales dropped 14%. I believe a communication breakdown between sales associates and buyers has contributed to the decline.

In our company, most sales associates do not know their buyers. The sales associates I spoke with felt intimidated by and did not communicate with the buyers. The buyers, on the other hand, aren't receiving the information they need to purchase the merchandise that the customers want.

In this report, I'll provide more information on the problem and offer a solution that I believe will help improve communication and increase sales.

Statement of the Problem

Simply stated, the problem is a lack of communication between the buyers and sales associates. The sales associates, who work directly with the customers, know what shoppers are looking for and what they request. Now that the company is emphasizing customer satisfaction, it is more important than ever to have the merchandise that customers want.

For example, I have worked in the Young Men's department for 18 months, yet no buyer has asked me what my customers want. I've noticed that the buyers for Young Men's clothing are middle-aged men who are busy trying to get the best clothing deals they can, rather than finding out what the customers are requesting. As a result, we get good prices on clothing, but customers aren't buying because the merchandise doesn't suit young male shoppers' tastes. Because I get direct feedback from the customers on their preferences, I'm in a good position to help buyers purchase clothing that will sell. Unfortunately, we have no formal way for me to communicate with the buyers.

SAMPLE REPORT (continued)

Proposed Solution

To ensure that our customers receive the merchandise they want, we need to set up a regular exchange of information between the buyers and the sales associates. This can be accomplished by having regular meetings and by conversations over the phone.

We could arrange meetings, which would require each department's buyers to go to three stores monthly. Since there are 22 stores and two buyers per department, one buyer would visit each department about once every quarter. The meetings could be held in either the department's office or in the store training room.

Between meetings, I recommend that sales associates call their buyers directly at least monthly.

Advantages and Disadvantages of Adopting the Solution

To save time and costs, I considered communication solely by mail or telephone, but I rejected these options because they lack timeliness, direct feedback, and face-to-face interaction. Without meeting and brainstorming, the quality of the discussions is diminished. Sales associates are used to working directly with customers, and they feel more comfortable meeting face-to-face.

Communicating by mail would be less expensive than having meetings, but it creates a time delay in any interaction. This delay could frustrate both the associates and the buyers, which could lead to reluctance in writing and a return to the original problem.

Communication only during the meetings between buyers and sales associates would not be effective simply because of infrequent interaction (every 3–4 months).

Other benefits of improving communication between the buyers and the sales associates follow:

- Improved customer relations because we'll be responding to their merchandise requests
- A mutually beneficial working relationship between buyers and sales associates
- Increased sales because we'll be stocking merchandise that customers want

An added benefit could result when the buyers actually visit the departments of the sales associates and see the floor plans. With their merchandising experience, buyers might suggest alternative ways of arranging the products on the floor to increase customer traffic and encourage sales.

With direct interaction between buyers and sales associates leading to more frequent communication, we should notice a better and more productive working relationship.

Conclusion

Our sales have dropped 14% in the last quarter, and I believe that lack of communication between sales associates and buyers has contributed to the drop-off. To resolve the lack of communication, I recommend establishing regular meetings and telephone conversations between buyers and sales associates as described in this report.

If communication between sales associates and buyers takes place, buyers should begin to understand the needs of customers through their sales associates. From this, customer satisfaction will increase as well as sales.

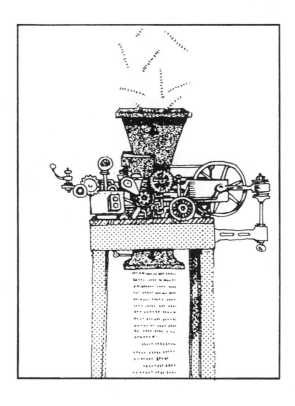

REVIEW OF SAMPLE REPORT

By using the five headings, Gary developed his thoughts within a well organized framework. Let's take another look.

1. **Overview:** In this section, Gary mentions a problem and suggests a possible cause and effect (that is, the communication breakdown is likely contributing to a decline in sales). Gary also previews the remainder of his report.

2. **Statement of the Problem:** Here, Gary states that the lack of communication between the sales staff and the buyers results in customers not getting the merchandise they would buy. He develops this section by providing an example to support his claim.

3. **Proposed Solution:** Gary offers that the company can improve communication by setting up regular meetings and telephone communication between buyers and sales staff.

4. **Advantages and Disadvantages of Proposed Solution:** To show that he has explored the problem, Gary mentions alternatives to his proposed solution; he then explains why he rejected the alternatives as not superior to his solution. This section is important in anticipating and overcoming the reader's objections or questions (that is, the reader is likely to say, "But what if we did 'A' instead of 'B'?" or "But did Gary consider this over that?").

5. **Conclusion/recommendation:** Gary's paragraph briefly summarizes his report and specifically restates his recommendation.

As mentioned previously, an added advantage to organizing your reports using subheadings such as these is that they not only make your report easier to write, they make your report easier to read. In this example, Gary's boss can skim the subheadings and select a section to find the specific information he needs.

SAMPLE FEASIBILITY STUDY

Now, we will look at the follow-up to this problem-solution report. This time we will conduct a feasibility study. Cheryl Babcock's assignment is to study the feasibility of starting regular meetings between sales associates and buyers. She will use Gary Pence's problem-solution report as a starting point. Her format follows the feasibility study headings suggested on page 26.

MEMORANDUM

TO: *Stewart Jensen, CEO*

FROM: *Cheryl Babcock*

DATE: *November 18, 19XX*

RE: *Studying the Feasibility of Establishing Regular Meetings Between Sales Associates and Buyers*

Overview

At your request, my staff and I have concluded our study of the feasibility of our sales associates and buyers meeting regularly. In our meeting last month, we all agreed with Gary that lack of communication has contributed to the decline of sales.

The primary purpose of this study is to explore the logistics of establishing the meetings. To do this, we've included a description of the details of our project, drawn conclusions to our findings, and offered recommendations for implementing the meetings.

Background

According to our financial statement, our sales dropped 14% last quarter—and our accounting department reports another decline so far this quarter. Gary reports that a communication breakdown between sales associates and buyers has contributed to the decline. From his experience as a sales associate, he states that most sales associates do not know their buyers, and those who do feel intimidated by and do not communicate with the buyers.

The problems created by this lack of communication lead to the buyers not receiving the information they need from the sales associates to purchase the merchandise that the customers want.

SAMPLE FEASIBILITY STUDY (continued)

<u>Project Details</u>

Approach: *Our first step was to survey a cross section of buyers and sales associates to find out their perceptions. We sent a questionnaire to the 125 sales associates and 44 buyers in the men's wear departments. Surprisingly, we received 111 responses from the associates and 34 responses from the buyers. Generally, in surveys we consider a 40% response to be excellent. Our responses with this survey ranged from 77% to 88%. A consensus agreed that regular communication between the two groups would help improve merchandise selection and display.*

After we reviewed the responses to our survey, we interviewed by telephone a cross section of both buyers and sales associates. Then we compiled and analyzed their comments. The results of both the survey and the interviews will be sent to you next week.

Findings: *The majority agreed that regular communication would improve the relationship between the two groups and should increase sales. The problem was how to set up the new communication system. We studied the possibility of communication by telephone because it would be faster and less expensive than any other method.*

Communicating by mail or fax would be cost effective, but mailing creates a time delay and not every men's wear department has a fax machine yet—although we understand that each department will have a fax machine by early 19XX.

Communication through meetings between buyers and sales associates would accomplish more than by any other method simply because both groups respond well through face-to-face interaction. We encounter time and cost problems if we consider meeting more than every 3–4 months, and meeting less often would not permit the regular dialogue we need between the two groups.

<u>Conclusion</u>

To ensure that our customers receive the merchandise they want, we agree with Gary that we need to set up a regular exchange of information between the buyers and the sales associates.

As a result of our survey and interviews, we can accomplish this new communication by combining media—having regular quarterly meetings and semi-monthly conversations over the phone.

If communication between sales associates and buyers takes place as Gary suggested, buyers should begin to understand the needs of customers through their sales associates. Responses to our survey suggested that customer satisfaction will increase as well as sales.

Recommendations

Regular meetings would require each department's buyers to go to three stores quarterly. When the buyers visit the stores, they will also have an opportunity to suggest alternative ways of displaying the merchandise. Generally, sales associates have fewer than 5 years' experience in merchandising while buyers have an average of 9 years' experience. We believe that each store will benefit from the buyers' merchandising knowledge.

Between meetings, sales associates should call their buyers semi-monthly, and by early 19XX, when each department gets its own fax machine, buyers who are in the field can keep in touch with the associates.

With your approval, we will draft a memo to all buyers and sales associates and include a tentative schedule of meetings for next year.

With direct interaction between buyers and sales associates leading to more frequent communication, we should notice a more productive working relationship and, most important, increased sales in future quarters.

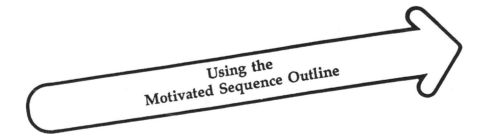

Using the Motivated Sequence Outline

SAMPLE REPORT USING THE MOTIVATED SEQUENCE OUTLINE

Ken Castle, manager of the creative graphics department at Phoenix Graphix, is writing a memorandum report to Bill Sayers, president of the company, to persuade him to hire a new camera-ready technician. Here is Ken's report, which follows the Motivated Sequence Outline introduced earlier.

MEMORANDUM
TO: BILL SAYERS
FROM: KEN CASTLE
RE: EXPANDING THE CREATIVE GRAPHICS DEPARTMENT
DATE: SEPTEMBER 13, 19XX

ATTENTION

Creativity and professionalism are qualities that enabled Phoenix Graphix to double its sales last year. We can continue to increase our sales in the creative graphics department this year if we hire another creative, professional person.

NEED

When we first developed the creative graphics department five years ago, we had two employees—and just enough work to keep them busy. Since then, sales for Phoenix Graphix have been steadily increasing and, according to our accountants, the creative graphics department has been responsible for 45% of that growth. We're confident that we can continue growing, but we need to consider hiring a camera-ready technician to complete our staff.

SATISFACTION

Fortunately, I recently interviewed a woman named Adrienne Smith, who has experience in camera-ready art and sales, and a degree in Business Administration with a minor in Commercial Art. Adrienne would be a perfect fit for our needs.

VISUALIZATION

After interviewing Adrienne I was excited by her blend of skills. Her four years' experience in paste-up and camera-ready art will help us better serve clients. No longer will we have to hire outside vendors for this kind of work. Her background in sales and training is a bonus. As we grow, she can help train others to prepare camera-ready art.

ACTION

Given the opportunity, I believe that Adrienne would contribute substantially to the creative graphics department's growth and development. I recommend we hire her immediately—before some other company discovers her!

I will call you on Thursday, the 15th, to discuss the possibility of offering Adrienne a position.

EDITING YOUR WRITTEN REPORTS

After you have developed a complete draft of your report, your next step is to edit it—preferably when you are fresh and objective, after you have taken a break from writing it.

Following is an example of an edited memorandum report. The edited changes are handwritten.

MEMORANDUM

TO: Janet Smith

FROM: Susan Fahs

RE: Evaluation of Your Report to Management

DATE: May 7, 19XX

~~I am writing to you about~~ Your report, ~~which~~ includes, ~~lots~~ *a lot* of good information, and you've generally organized ~~this~~ *it* well ~~well~~ (chapter sequence), but it will be clearer and more concise if you do the following:

1. Make sure you keep your paragraphs cohesive and coherent. See my comments regarding some paragraphs not tying in well with preceding information.

2. Choose your words carefully. Do they ~~say~~ *convey* exactly what you mean? For example, do you really mean "state the scope"? Would "specify" or "define" the scope be more accurate?

3. *Avoid* Pronoun shift. For example, you use third person (a manager) in the same sentence as second person, "you."

4. Omit needless words and repetitive phrases.

5. *Use* ~~Shorter~~ sentences *which* ~~are~~ often better than longer ones.

6. Avoid using absolutes. For example, *if you say* "things will go wrong," ~~is awfully~~ *can you be certain?* ~~strong and perhaps not necessarily so.~~

7. Find an appropriate conversational (not colloquial) tone and use it consistently. For example, "this is where you do the things that need to be done" _sounds_ too casual.

8. Read your report aloud to apply the conversational tone test. Does it sound clear?

9. Add examples to help clarify and provide support.

10. Buy and read William Zinsser's <u>The Art of Writing Well</u>—it's terrific, and ~~it's~~ one of the single best sources of writing I've seen.

I've made ~~more~~ detailed comments on the first few pages of the report. For sake of time, these comments will probably apply to the rest of your report. Please ~~come~~ see me ~~anytime~~ if you have questions.

COMPLETING YOUR REPORTS

As you edit your report, you will want to add examples or explanations to clarify fuzzy sections, delete redundant information, reorganize sections that do not flow well, apply the conversation test to *hear* if your report sounds natural, and proofread for grammatical, spelling or typographical errors.

When you complete the first draft, step back, look over your work and ask yourself these questions:

- Do I need to put additional information in an Appendix? [Some information does not fit neatly into the body of a report, perhaps because it unnecessarily interrupts the continuity, but you can refer to the information that you have included in an Appendix.]

- Have I been generous with white space? [Part of your work as a writer is to make your report easy to read. One way to do that is to use white space to break up blocks of text.]

- Could I add graphics to make my examples clearer and more interesting? [Visuals work well to clarify information that is technical or otherwise difficult to explain. Charts and graphs—especially in color—also attract and help retain the reader's attention and interest.]

- Have I supported my claims and arguments? [Remember that saying something without evidence tells your reader you need to do more homework.]

Completing your reports also involves preparing a title page; a letter of transmittal, if necessary; a table of contents if your report is longer than eight pages; and an appendix, if you need to add supporting information.

On the following three pages are examples of title pages based on reports we have seen in earlier chapters. Title pages work well on formal reports and proposals, but you normally do not need them on informal reports and proposals.

SAMPLE TITLE PAGE

REPORT ON NEW SEMINAR: "HOW TO MARKET OUR SERVICES"

Prepared for Steve Johnson
Personnel Director, ABC Corporation

September 13, 19XX

by

Carolyn Carter
Accounting Manager
ABC Corporation

SAMPLE TITLE PAGE

FOR FREMONT STORES, INC.

REPORT TO REDUCE COMMUNICATION PROBLEMS

AND INCREASE SALES

Presented to
Stewart Jensen, CEO
Fremont Stores, Inc.

by

Gary Pence, Senior Sales Associate
Orange County Store

Los Angeles, California
October 23, 19XX

SAMPLE TITLE PAGE

FEASIBILITY STUDY
ESTABLISHING REGULAR MEETINGS BETWEEN
SALES ASSOCIATES AND BUYERS
FOR FREMONT STORES, INC.

Stewart Jensen, CEO

by
Cheryl Babcock
Director, Marketing & Communications

November 18, 19XX

P A R T

III

Writing Winning Proposals

DEVELOPING YOUR IDEAS

Similar to reports, once you have outlined your proposals, you will need to complete your first draft. Following is an example of another way to organize and develop a proposal.

1. OVERVIEW OR EXECUTIVE SUMMARY—*convey your main ideas clearly and concisely*

2. OBJECTIVES—*identify their needs*

3. SOLUTIONS—*identify what you can do for them*

4. ABOUT YOUR COMPANY—*explain why they should select you*

5. FEES—*state what they can expect to pay for your services or product*

6. APPENDIX—*add any other relevant or supporting piece of information to enhance your proposal.*

Beginning on page 58 is an example of a proposal developed using these headings. In this proposal, English Associates responded to an RFP (Request for Proposal) from Northwest Mutual Insurance Company to set up communication training programs for its employees.

Sample Report

A PROPOSAL TO PROVIDE COMMUNICATION TRAINING
FOR NORTHWEST MUTUAL INSURANCE COMPANY

by

SHARON ENGLISH

ENGLISH ASSOCIATES

June 19XX

[OVERVIEW]

Thank you for providing English Associates with this opportunity to propose consulting services to assist Northwest Mutual Insurance Company (NMIC) in setting up communication training programs for its employees.

Our proposal demonstrates our understanding of NMIC and its needs, describes English Associates' approach and qualifications, introduces our staff and explains our estimated fees. We are committed to providing timely responsive and cost-effective service, while we help you set up training programs to improve the interpersonal skills of your sales associates.

[OBJECTIVES]

BACKGROUND

Founded in 1986, NMIC is an insurance company providing professional liability insurance. Recently, NMIC management has perceived a need for improved communication performance on the part of supervisory and middle-management sales associates to strengthen relationships between them and their subordinates.

NMIC's management has asked for help in establishing regular training programs for all employees, to begin later this year.

[SOLUTIONS]

OUR APPROACH

We propose to work with you to help you achieve management's goal of developing more effective employee communication. More specifically, we believe that the following method should be effective in producing stronger interpersonal skills for your employees:

Interactive Training: Employees learn to improve their interpersonal skills best by actively participating in the training through role playing, discussing case studies and identifying their communicating styles through self-analysis excercises.

SAMPLE PROPOSAL (continued)

With this approach, instructors act as facilitators rather than lecturers. Group feedback and discussion reinforces learning.

Content: To achieve your goals, we recommend covering the following topics:

- Identifying each employee's communication style

- Discovering strategies to manage conflict

- Learning how to self-monitor effectively

- Reading non-verbal signals

- Conducting more productive meetings

Format: This 8-hour course is best suited for a maximum of 16 employees participating in each session.

[ABOUT YOUR COMPANY]

OUR COMPANY

To accomplish your objectives, our engagement team of experienced consultants is the critical—and most distinguishing—factor in our ability to provide high quality consulting services.

English Associates differs from other consulting firms for these main reasons:

- Extensive knowledge of and familiarity with your organization and industry, because of our long-standing relationship as your primary communication consultants

- Twenty-five years' experience in employee communication—longer than any other local consultant

- A professional staff committed to providing responsive and cost-effective service

[FEES]

OUR FEES

English Associates will provide all materials needed for this 8-hour course, including participant handbooks, videotapes and playback units, exercises, case studies and other visual aids. The cost of each program is $2,250.

Any out-of-pocket expenses (such as travel, hotel, photocopying and telephone) will be billed separately. We don't expect the out-of-pocket expenses to exceed $1,000.

SAMPLE PROPOSAL (continued)

[APPENDIX]

RESUMES

Sharon English

Sharon has over 12 years of business communication experience including conducting meeting leader training sessions and focus groups, teaching presentation skills, critiquing presentations of other professionals, writing texts, speeches and scripts, and producing informational videotapes.

Prior to joining English Associates, Sharon taught business writing, public speaking and interpersonal communication at the college level.

Sharon received a Bachelor of Science degree in Social Sciences from San Francisco State University and a Master of Arts degree in Communication from San Diego State University. Sharon is a member of the Speech Communication Association, the Western States Communication Association and the International Association of Business Communicators.

Sarah Connell

Sarah specializes in providing consulting services to clients in Human Resources Management. She brings to consulting over 15 years of management of all aspects of the Human Resources function with four major corporations.

Sarah's recent assignments include developing and implementing a fourteen week training course on effective presentation skills and conducting a series of seminars on conflict management for a department of the U.S. Government.

Sarah graduated from the University of Washington and is a member of The Society of Human Resource Management.

EDITING YOUR WRITTEN PROPOSALS

As soon as you complete the first draft of your proposal, set it aside for awhile; then, return to it with a refreshed perspective and begin editing.

The sample proposal shown on pages 64–67 is in the final stages of editing. Note the handwritten edited comments.

Sample Edited Proposal

SAMPLE EDITED PROPOSAL

A PROPOSAL TO PROVIDE
COMMUNICATION TRAINING ∧ *SERVICES*

FOR NORTHWEST MUTUAL INSURANCE COMPANY

by

~~SHARON ENGLISH,~~ *← Delete name before final printing*

ENGLISH ASSOCIATES

June 19XX

make letter format {

Thank you for providing English Associates with ~~this~~ [you] opportunity to propose consulting services to assist ~~Northwest Mutual Insurance Company (NMIC)~~ in setting up communication training programs for ~~its~~ [your] employees.

Our proposal demonstrates our understanding of your needs, describes English Associates' approach, introduces our training team, and ~~explains~~ [lists] our estimated fees. We are committed to providing timely and responsive service, while we help you set up training programs to improve the interpersonal skills of your sales associates.

We believe an excellent opportunity exists for us to work together to help achieve your goals. We welcome the opportunity to discuss this proposal with you or to provide you with additional information. ~~you need.~~ If you have questions, please call me at 772-2265.

BACKGROUND

Founded in 1986, NMIC is an insurance company providing professional liability insurance. Recently, NMIC management has perceived a need for improved communication performance on the part of supervisory and middle-management ~~sales associates~~ to strengthen relationships between them and their subordinates.

NMIC's management has asked for help in establishing regular training programs for all employees, to begin later this year.

OUR APPROACH

Clarify {

Based on our experience, establishing specific objectives will help satisfy your organization's prupose. Our approach is to help ~~you~~ achieve management's goal of developing more effective employee communication. More specifically, ~~we believe that~~ the following method will produce more effective interpersonal skills for your employees.

Interactive Training: Employees learn to improve their interpersonal skills best by actively participating in the training through role playing, discussing case studies and identifying their communicating stlyles through self-analysis exercises.

With this approach, instructors act as facilitators rather than lecturers. Group feedback and discussion reinforces learning.

SAMPLE EDITED PROPOSAL (continued)

Content: To achieve your goals, we recommend covering the following topics:

- Identifying each employee's communication style
- Discovering strategies to manage conflict
- Learning how to self-monitor effectively
- Reading non-verbal signals
- Conducting more productive meetings

Format: This 8-hour course is best suited for a maximum of 16 employees participating in each session.

OUR COMPANY

To provide you with high quality consulting services, our people are the critical—and most distinguishing—factor. To accomplish your objectives, we have selected a training team of our two most experienced consultants.

English Associates differs from other consulting firms because of our:

- Extensive knowledge of and familiarity with your organization and industry, because of our long-standing relationship as your primary communication consultants

- Professional staff committed to providing responsive and cost-effective service

Our philosophy is to emphasize what's best for NMIC rather than what's best for English Associates. In the past, you've experienced firsthand the advantages of this approach. For example, teaching your human resources staff to conduct their own annual employee meetings, you were able to save the time and expense of bringing in outside consultants, and you provided growth opportunities for your staff.

OUR FEES

English Associates will provide all materials needed for this 8-hour course, including participant handbooks, videotapes and playback units, exercises, case studies and other visual aids. The cost of each program is $2,250. *Add information on out-of-pocket costs (travel, meals, printing)*

RESUMES

Sharon English

Sharon has over 12 years of business communication experience including conducting training sessions and focus groups, teaching presentation skills, critiquing presentations of other professionals, writing scripts and producing informational videotapes.

Prior to joining English Associates, Sharon taught business writing, public speaking and interpersonal communication at the college level.

Sharon received a Bachelor of Science degree in Social Sciences from San Francisco State University and a Master of Arts degree in Communication from San Diego State University. Sharon is a member of the International Association of Business Communicators.

Sarah Connell

Sarah specializes in providing consulting services to clients in Human Resources Management. She brings to consulting over 15 years of management of all aspects of the Human Relations function with four major corporations.

Sarah's recent assignments include developing and implementing a fourteen week training course on effective presentation skills and conducting a series of seminars on conflict management for a department of the U.S. Government.

Sarah graduated from the University of Washington and is a member of The Society for Human Resource Management.

COMPLETING YOUR PROPOSALS

When you review your developed proposal, check to see if you need to add examples or explanation to clarify sections, delete redundant information, reorganize sections that do not flow well, apply the conversation test to *hear* if your proposal sounds natural, and proofread for grammatical, spelling or typographical errors.

Look over your work and ask yourself these questions:

• Do I need to put additional or supporting information in an Appendix?

• Have I been generous with white space? [Remember that because proposals are persuasive, the more you layout your information to encourage your reader to continue reading, the more likely your reader's response will be favorable.]

• Could I add graphics to make my examples clearer and more interesting? [Visuals work well to clarify information that is technical or otherwise difficult to explain. Charts and graphs—especially in color—also attract and help retain the reader's attention and interest.]

• Have I supported my claims and arguments? [Remember that saying something without evidence tells your reader you need to do more homework.]

Beginning on the next page is the first page of a sample proposal. Each section is labeled and briefly described to help explain the reasons for including it. Note that the sections are different from the ones presented earlier.

As you take a second look at this proposal, ask yourself the questions above, and write any suggestions you would make in the space provided following each section.

[INTRODUCTORY OR COVER LETTER—EXPLAINS THE PURPOSE OF THE PROPOSAL AND PROVIDES AN OVERVIEW OF THE CONTENTS]

May 2, 19XX

Ms. Jan Anderson, Buyer
Widgit, Inc.
10550 Talbert Avenue
Fountain Valley, CA 92728-0850

Dear Ms. Anderson:

We appreciate the opportunity to expand our services to Widgit, Inc. by helping you prepare medical benefit handbooks for your employees. Currently, we are preparing benefit booklets for several of our clients, ranging in size from 200 to 10,000 employees.

Based on the scope of this project, we've listed the major stages involved, provided a proposed timeline for each step in the process, and included cost estimates for MLF Company's consulting services. We have also included cost estimates for the major outside vendor services that we expect will be required.

Please call me at (415/953-3255) with your questions about this project or the proposed services that we have described. After you have had a chance to review our proposal, I will call you to see how we might best proceed. We're eager to begin helping you create your new benefits handbooks for your employees.

Sincerely,

Susan Hunt

/slh
Enclosures

Suggested Revisions:

_____

_____

_____

_____

_____

_____

COMPLETING YOUR PROPOSALS (continued)

[EXPLAINING HOW MUCH TIME IS REQUIRED TO COMPLETE THE PROCESS HELPS THE PROSPECT UNDERSTAND THE TIME COMMITMENT FOR EACH STEP OF THE PROCESS, AND WHAT HIS OR HER ROLE IS IN THE PROJECT.]

PROPOSED TIMELINE

The following timeline outlines the expected completion dates for the major steps of the process.

Assumptions: Project Start Date: May 20, 19XX
Final Statements due by September 30, 19XX

Completion Date	Event
May 24, 19XX	Confirm all benefit plans to be included on the statement and the source of data from WI.
June 15, 19XX	Finalize statement text and artwork for approval by WI.
June 30, 19XX	Finalize individual participants' data to be provided by WI to MLF Company.
July 12, 19XX	Provide test data for selected employees to MLF Company.
August 1, 19XX	Provide final data tapes for the selected benefit plans to MLF Company.
September 1, 19XX	Data edit report to WI for corrections. MLF Company completes and WI approves the integrating, editing and verifying of data to be used for statement production.
September 25, 19XX	WI employee benefit statements are printed and mailed to employees.

Suggested Revisions:

_____

_____

_____

_____

_____

[TO GIVE THIS PROSPECTIVE CLIENT A BETTER UNDERSTANDING OF THE PROCESS, SUSAN HUNT INCLUDES A DESCRIPTION OF THE MAJOR STAGES. NOT ONLY IS THIS INFORMATIVE, BUT IT DEFINES THE SCOPE OF THE PROJECT, AND IT HELPS SUPPORT THE FEES.]

STAGES OF THE BENEFIT BOOKLET PROCESS

Based on our experience, the following steps describe the typical major stages of producing benefit booklets.

1. Determine the benefits to be included and identify the sources of data.

2. Draft and format the statement text and list the benefits in the desired order.

3. Design artwork and graphs, if applicable, for the statement cover and inside pages.

4. Combine the text with each employee's data and test for accuracy.

5. Print and distribute the booklets.

Suggested Revisions:

_____

_____

_____

_____

_____

_____

_____

_____

_____

_____

_____

_____

COMPLETING YOUR PROPOSALS (continued)

[WHILE FEES SHOULD NOT BE THE DETERMINING FACTOR IN SELECTING ONE FIRM OVER ANOTHER, SUSAN HUNT PROVIDES AN ESTIMATE OF COSTS FOR HER WORK, TO HELP PREVENT ANY UNPLEASANT SURPRISES WHEN THE CLIENT RECEIVES HER BILL.]

ESTIMATED COSTS

Following are estimated costs for producing WI's benefit booklets. Mailing costs are included in printing charges.

	Estimated Costs
1. Develop and design booklets, including organizing and coordinating each step of the process, writing text, and designing artwork	$14,000
2. Print 675 booklets and envelopes (2 color with cover)	$ 4,000
Total Estimated Costs	$18,000

Suggested Revisions:

_____

_____

_____

_____

_____

_____

_____

_____

_____

_____

_____

_____

_____

[TESTIMONIALS ARE NOT ALWAYS NECESSARY, BUT BY PROVIDING A LIST OF PEOPLE WHO CAN SPEAK ON HER BEHALF, SUSAN CAN BOLSTER HER CREDIBILITY.]

REFERENCES

1. ABC Inc.
   Human Resources Department
   2000 Fresno Street, Suite 200
   San Marine, CA 94577
   (415) 777-5223

   Contact: Janet Hughes

   We prepare comprehensive benefit booklets annually for 10,000 employees.

2. Grant Company
   6600 Oscar Drive
   Pleasant Valley, CA 94699
   (415) 828-0694

   Contact: Stan Brown
             Assistant to the President

   We prepare benefit booklets annually for 800 employees.

3. XYZ Technologies
   3199 First Street
   Fremont, CA 94333
   (408) 455-2855

   Contact: William Larsen
             Director of Human Resources

   We prepare benefits booklets annually for 2,000 employees.

Suggested Revisions:

_____

_____

_____

_____

_____

_____

SAMPLE PROPOSAL

On the following pages is a complete proposal that is more formal and technical as well as organized differently from the others you have seen in this book. For example, the proposal includes an overview letter followed by these sections: more information about the company, a description of the people who will be doing the work, fee estimates, and special strengths the company has to offer.

Take a few minutes to review this sample proposal. After you finish, put yourself in the place of the recipient, Enterprise Insurance Company, and answer the following questions:

1. How has Systems, Inc. written for the YOU perspective?

_____

_____

_____

2. How has Systems, Inc. convinced me they can do the job?

_____

_____

_____

3. What is effective about this proposal? Be specific.

_____

_____

_____

4. Specifically, what would I improve about this proposal?

_____

_____

_____

PROPOSAL TO PROVIDE CONSULTING SERVICES FOR

ENTERPRISE INSURANCE COMPANY

BY

SYSTEMS, INC.

July 12, 19XX

SAMPLE PROPOSAL (continued)

July 12, 19XX

Ms. Melanie Cody
Enterprise Insurance Company
777 San Marino Drive
San Diego, CA 90202

Dear Ms. Cody:

Re: Response to Request for Proposal

Thank you for providing Systems, Inc. with this opportunity to propose consulting services to assist you with an inventory control system for your national offices. This proposal describes our approach to inventory control and our qualifications to provide these services on behalf of Enterprise Insurance Company.

After reviewing your Request for Proposal (RFP), we believe that your objectives center on finding a consultant with the following qualifications:

- National credibility;

- Local capabilities committed to providing responsive and cost-effective service;

- Computer systems tailored for inventory control; and

- Knowledgeable and innovative people.

This proposal will demonstrate that Systems, Inc. has these qualifications. We're committed to helping you achieve successful inventory control while providing timely, responsive, and cost-effective service.

In the sections following this overview, you will find information about our company, people, and special strengths, and the ways we can work with you to help solve your inventory problems.

OUR NATIONAL CLIENTS AND LOCAL CAPABILITIES

Nationally, we serve a wide range of clients, including the following:

- Fremont Transtech
- Acme Corporation
- Fidelity Inc.
- Weston & Weston
- Wyatt Limited
- Smithson Corporation

Locally, our Los Angeles office offers a full range of consulting services provided by a professional staff of over 80 consultants. We are excited about this opportunity to contribute to your efficiency and success by becoming your consultant.

OUR TECHNOLOGY

Systems, Inc. is a leader in applying computer technology to help streamline inventory control. In response to your request, we are proposing to use **ICS**™, which is an inventory control system that is both flexible and user-friendly. We would be pleased to demonstrate this system to show you how we can meet your inventory control needs.

OUR PEOPLE

We believe you will find that our people are the critical—and distinguishing—factor in our ability to provide you with high quality and effective inventory control services.

Experience and technical competence are the primary considerations we use in selecting our project teams. To best serve you, we have drawn from the experience of our Firm to assemble our most qualified people to set up and assist you with your inventory control systems.

* * * *

We appreciate the opportunity to present our proposed services, and we believe an excellent opportunity exists for us to work together to help achieve your goals.

After you review this proposal, please call either John Montgomery at (815) 555-3022 or Dave Fields at (815) 555-3333 if you have questions. We are eager to meet with you to present our ideas to help you better control your inventory.

Sincerely,

Julie Mechling
SYSTEMS, INC.

SAMPLE PROPOSAL (continued)

MORE ABOUT SYSTEMS, INC.

Systems, Inc. provides a wide range of highly specialized professional business services to clients throughout the United States, many of whom are Fortune 500 companies. Nationally, the firm has 125 partners and over 4,000 employees in 30 cities. The Los Angeles office includes over 50 professional and administrative staff. As a result of our commitment to providing responsive service, we have grown to become one of the largest consulting firms in the United States.

REFERENCES

Fred Henry
Manager
ACME Inc.
2900 March Street
San Marino, California 94444
(415) 563-1311

Systems, Inc. has served ACME for over 25 years.

Ms. Frances Kennedy
Director
Kelly-Smith Company
200 International Drive
Chicago, Illinois 60000
(718) 366-9867

Systems, Inc. has provided consulting services to Kelly-Smith since 1987.

Mr. Edward Brunnel
Director
Burgess-Kingman, Inc.
810 Capital Road
Sunnyside, California 94577
(408) 370-8676

Systems, Inc. has provided consulting services to Burgess-Kingman since 1987. Currently, the plan covers 1,800 participants. Burgess-Kingman uses ICS™'s on-line inventory system.

YOUR PROPOSED PROJECT TEAM

Our work for you would be under the general direction of John Montgomery, Partner. John will allocate those resources needed to serve Enterprise Insurance Company. Dave Fields will directly supervise the team we select to support the ongoing operation of the inventory system.

To assist you in assessing the qualifications of the team that will be assigned to the Enterprise Insurance Company engagement, following are brief descriptions of each individual's resume.

Depending on the scope of the work to be performed and staff level needed to complete the required tasks, we assign staff with appropriate skills and experience to help ensure that they will work well with your employees.

Our style is to take the initiative to bring useful and innovative ideas to your attention. In addition, we are flexible: depending on your needs, we are available to do as much or as little as you request.

Project Team

Dave Fields, Project Coordinator

Dave is a Manager in the Los Angeles office of Systems, Inc.

Within the field of consulting, Dave's background is varied and extensive. Dave's academic training is in human resources and includes a BA from Ferguson College and graduate degrees from UCLA. Prior to joining SI in 1980, Dave was an Instructor at Ferguson College.

Angela Baty, Computer Technology Team Leader

Angela is an Associate Manager in Systems, Inc. She is a member of the Systems Technology team, with primary emphasis in implementing inventory systems for our clients. Angela brings over 12 years of technical experience to this project.

Angela is a member of the Human Resources Systems Professionals (HRSP). She received an MS degree in Computer Science from the University of Southern California.

SAMPLE PROPOSAL (continued)

Susan Reynolds, Inventory Systems Specialist

Susan is a Specialist in the Los Angeles office of Systems, Inc. She has over 4 years of technical experience in implementing systems. Susan received a BS in Computer Technology from CalTech.

FEE ESTIMATES

SI will provide you with complete services for the installation of your inventory control system. Our proposal represents a firm commitment to deliver the services described for the proposed fees.

The fees described below are based on the time required to complete the engagement and on the classification of the assigned professional staff.

We estimate the fee to complete the inventory control system set-up, conversion and testing, and training to be $65,000. A more detailed description of this fee follows:

System Set-up—Set up services include design and customization of the inventory system. $30,000

Conversion—Transferring your current inventory information to our system will require coordination and careful control. Our fee includes both transferring the data and testing it for accuracy. 20,000

Training—Our staff will train your employees to use the new inventory control system through one-on-one instruction and with user manuals. After system installation, we will remain involved and provide assistance as required by your employees. 15,000

Total $65,000

OUR SPECIAL STRENGTHS

SI has extensive national resources to support our consultants in serving our clients. Our systems were developed by senior people in our Chicago office. These people, who are the architects of the system, will be available to respond to your special needs and requests. Additionally, the following information highlights other special strengths we offer to you:

- People who know your business and who can help you to set up and convert your inventory data and train your people to confidently and accurately run your system;

- High quality, consistent service, ensured by internal quality control procedures;

- An established record of providing high quality consulting services timely and cost efficiently. We encourage you to call our references for more specific information regarding our track record with them; and

- A large and highly qualified local staff in Los Angeles.

Above all else, we offer our commitment to quality. Because accurate inventory control is essential to your credibility with your customers, we are committed to working with you to establish an effective and efficient system that assists you in maintaining a high level of accuracy in your inventory control.

SAMPLE PROPOSAL (continued)

As you reviewed the proposal and responded to the questions, did you feel more knowledgeable about what makes a proposal effective?

This brings us to a final suggestion: read as many proposals and reports as you can and study them. Put yourself in the place of the prospective client, and ask yourself the questions you responded to on page 74.

Once you are more comfortable with your capabilities in reviewing proposals and reports, you will be well on the way to feeling more comfortable writing effective proposals and reports.

The suggestions in the next section should help you feel more confident when your next assignment is to pull together a proposal and report.

P A R T

IV

Review Checklist

REVIEW

The following information should help you keep your priorities in mind the next time you need to prepare a proposal or report.

1. Prepare to write:
- Know your audience and their needs.
- Know your product and service.

2. Review the basics:
- Keep your writing natural and conversational.
- Omit needless words.
- Avoid using clichés.
- Remember the ''YOU'' perspective.

3. Choose an appropriate tone:
- Apply the conversation test.

4. Use a consistent style:
- Your style tells your reader a lot about you.

5. Edit to enhance your writing:
- Edit ruthlessly to refine and polish your drafts.

6. Add final polish:
- Add graphs and charts to help explain especially technical information.
- Proofread at least twice to make sure your report or proposal is free of typographical errors.

Congratulations! You should feel better prepared for your next report or proposal.

Remember: many people believe that their writing skills are adequate for their job; then they learn they have acquired bad writing habits that are difficult to break.

Writing is a process. It is often hard work even for good writers. And as with most skills, you must practice, practice, practice. Good luck!

NOTES

NOTES

NOW AVAILABLE FROM
CRISP PUBLICATIONS

Books • Videos • CD Roms • Computer-Based Training Products

Subject Areas Include:

Management

Human Resources

Communication Skills

Personal Development

Marketing/Sales

Organizational Development

Customer Service/Quality

Computer Skills

Small Business and Entrepreneurship

Adult Literacy and Learning

Life Planning and Retirement

CRISP WORLDWIDE DISTRIBUTION

English language books are distributed worldwide. Major international distributors include:

ASIA/PACIFIC

Australia/New Zealand: In Learning, PO Box 1051, Springwood QLD, Brisbane, Australia 4127   Tel: 61-7-3-841-2286, Facsimile: 61-7-3-841-1580
ATTN: Messrs. Gordon

Singapore: 85, Genting Lane, Guan Hua Warehouse Bldng #05-01, Singapore 349569   Tel: 65-749-3389, Facsimile: 65-749-1129
ATTN: Evelyn Lee

Japan: Phoenix Associates Co., LTD., Mizuho Bldg. 3-F, 2-12-2, Kami Osaki, Shinagawa-Ku, Tokyo 141   Tel: 81-33-443-7231, Facsimile: 81-33-443-7640
ATTN: Mr. Peter Owans

CANADA

Reid Publishing, Ltd., Box 69559-109 Thomas Street, Oakville, Ontario Canada L6J 7R4.   Tel: (905) 842-4428, Facsimile: (905) 842-9327
ATTN: Mr. Stanley Reid

Trade Book Stores: *Raincoast Books,* 8680 Cambie Street, Vancouver, B.C., V6P 6M9   Tel: (604) 323-7100, Facsimile: (604) 323-2600
ATTN: Order Desk

EUROPEAN UNION

England: *Flex Training,* Ltd. 9-15 Hitchin Street, Baldock, Hertfordshire, SG7 6A, England   Tel: 44-1-46-289-6000, Facsimile: 44-1-46-289-2417
ATTN: Mr. David Willetts

INDIA

Multi-Media HRD, Pvt., Ltd., National House, Tulloch Road, Appolo Bunder, Bombay, India 400-039   Tel: 91-22-204-2281, Facsimile: 91-22-283-6478
ATTN: Messrs. Aggarwal

SOUTH AMERICA

Mexico: *Grupo Editorial Iberoamerica,* Nebraska 199, Col. Napoles, 03810 Mexico, D.F.   Tel: 525-523-0994, Facsimile: 525-543-1173
ATTN: Señor Nicholas Grepe

SOUTH AFRICA

Alternative Books, Unit A3 Micro Industrial Park, Hammer Avenue, Stridom Park, Randburg, 2194 South Africa   Tel: 27-11-792-7730, Facsimile: 27-11-792-7787
ATTN: Mr. Vernon de Haas